How to Study

Arthur W. Kornhauser

How to Study

Suggestions for High School and College Students

THIRD EDITION

Revised by Diane M. Enerson

The University of Chicago Press
Chicago and London

The University of Chicago Press, Chicago 60637
The University of Chicago Press, Ltd., London
© 1924, 1937, 1993 by The University of Chicago
All rights reserved. Third edition published 1993
Printed in the United States of America
02 01   3 4 5

ISBN: 0-226-45118-6 (cloth)
ISBN: 0-226-45117-8 (paper)

Kornhauser, Arthur William, 1896–
    How to study : suggestions for high school and college students /
Arthur W. Kornhauser.—3rd ed. / revised by Diane M. Enerson.
        p.   cm.
    Includes bibliographical references (p.).
    1. Study, Method of.   I. Enerson, Diane M., 1946–   .   II. Title.
LB2395.K6   1993
378.1'702812—dc20   92-38217
                                                                CIP

Contents

Preface
to the Third Edition

IN his preface to the second edition of *How to Study*, Kornhauser began by noting that some measure and justification of his little book's intrinsic value are found in "[i]ts continued extensive use, twenty years after publication." Another half century has passed since he made this observation; yet this book seems no less appropriate now than it was then. Although I first learned of the book only recently, on several occasions since then I have mentioned it in groups of colleagues. Each time, at least one of those present—who have typically been somewhat older than myself—has responded by noting they remember it well, having used it as student themselves, and in fact still have their copy of it, a response that has both pleased and amused me. My interest in this little volume, though, is not so much that of someone who, like my colleagues, has cherished it for years but rather it is that of someone who searched for just such a book, discovered it only recently, and is pleased to help make it available to yet another generation of students who hope to become scholars, or at least more scholarly when they study.

During the six years I was director of Learning Resources and consultant in Study Skills in the College at the University of Chicago, I worked with hundreds of young people each year who were having difficulties making a successful transition from high school to college. For many of these students, the difficulties they were experiencing were centered in a single discipline, such as mathematics, or with a single skill, such as writing papers. But for the others, the problems were more global. Typically these were students for whom high school had been easy and success more or less automatic. Now in a new environment with more complex standards and expectations, they knew they should do something different, but they didn't know what. In other words, what they needed was a succinct and practical set of guidelines for studying that would help them gain conscious control over procedures and skills that while not wholly lacking were not always there when they needed them.

Early on—and on numerous occasions—during my years working in the College, I browsed through bookstore shelves in search of a current publication I could recommend to the students with whom I worked. What I hoped to find was a smallish, straightforward text with all the basics—no gimmicks, just gentle reminders and a clear articulation of what it means to be a student—a book I could use in conjunction with the sessions I had with these students. My searches, I regret to say, left me less than enthusiastic about the genre of how-to-study books. Most seemed overly pedantic, assuming far too little of the reader for the audience I had in mind. Although I did discover a few really valuable ones, such as *Style* (Williams), *Writing for Social Scientists* (Becker), and *Procrastination* (Burka and Yuen), and several others such as *How to Read a Book* (Adler) and of course *Elements of Style* (Strunk and White) that had withstood the test of time, none of these addressed the more fundamental issues of what it means to study. In the end, I contented myself with using bits and pieces from here and there and eventually gave up my search.

Thus, I was pleasantly surprised the first time I read through Kornhauser's book. The simple title, *How to Study*, had long since lost its charm through overuse, but its contents were a delight. In a mere fifty-five pages, the casual reader soon discovers all the basics for studying, and for doing so effectively. No gimmicks, just clear, simple advice. I never met Kornhauser, nor while I was at Chicago could I find anyone who had. So I can only guess about the kind of man he was. But on reading and rereading his book I would imagine that he was as unassuming and straightforward as the set of guidelines he sets out in it. Unlike many popular how-to texts, what Kornhauser says and how he says it makes clear that the responsibility for using and practicing the skills and habits he describes belongs to those who would hope to become more scholarly in their approach to studying. Not even a hint of panaceas here, just a detailed description of the habits that underlie effective learning.

In revising the text, therefore, I have tried to retain as much as possible of what I view as the book's— and probably Kornhauser's—character. Although the passage of time did necessitate a few changes, for the most part these have been limited to revisions of style and tone that eliminate some linguistic quirks which are no longer fashionable and which made the offered advice appear more dated than it really was.

These stylistic changes also include a few modifications of heading and format. What I have tried to do with these cosmetic revisions is appeal as successfully to students in the 1990s as Kornhauser's style appealed to earlier generations of college students. In the end, though, the only substantive revisions were, first, to the chapter on time management—where experience told me his advice might be a bit too succinct—and, second, to a chapter on speed reading, most of which I deleted (the remainder was subsumed within the chapter on reading effectively). Where virtually every other guideline and bit of advice Kornhauser offers his reader can be given greater weight by contemporary findings in psychology, the issue of speed reading is a far more controversial one. Further, many of the less controversial heuristics for increasing reading speed—for example, have a purpose or question in mind as you read—he covers elsewhere. Thus, it seemed prudent to simply delete this section but to suggest, for the interested student, other, more comprehensive treatments of the topic in a revised (and annotated) bibliography.

In the end, then, the intended readers of this book are, I hope, students roughly comparable to those for whom this book was originally written and for whom it proved useful over a half century ago. These students, like the ones I worked with at Chicago, are bright, capable, ambitious, and highly cognizant that they must study; they have had some earlier—if serendipitous—successes as students but now face courses in which skillful and effective mastery of the material does not come entirely naturally. There were many such students at Chicago, some of whom I had the pleasure of working with and some of whom I did not. Moreover, I am certain there are many, many more elsewhere as well, at private colleges and public universities, or even in many high schools throughout the country. Anywhere, in fact, where the courses they are taking require that they stretch beyond their existing study habits—some of which may have been developed fairly unconsciously. For many of these students, much of what Kornhauser has to say will seem obvious once they have read it. But that is just the point. The audience I have in mind more or less knows what it means to study, and it is the less part of that knowing that this little book addresses so successfully. It is my hope, then, that in editing the third edition of Kornhauser's book I will help to nurture yet another generation of students who will remember it fondly thirty-something years hence.

Diane M. Enerson
University Park, Pennsylvania
1993

Preface
to the Second Edition

Those booklet was originally prepared to meet the needs of Freshmen students in the School of Business of the University of Chicago. The material proved sufficiently general, however, to be widely applicable to other groups of college and high-school students. Its continued extensive use, twenty years after publication, appears to offer sufficient justification for the belief that it fills a real need.

In the present revised form the booklet remains essentially what it was. It still attempts to set forth very briefly a set of direct suggestions to help high-school and college students improve their study methods. A chapter has been added on methods for measuring reading improvement [now subsumed in chapter 5] in an effort to have students more actively *use* the suggestions of preceding chapters. Many other changes of wording and emphasis and numerous minor additions have been introduced in the interests of clarity and greater usefulness.

Sets of printed rules cannot, of course, take the place of more personal and continuous instruction in study methods by teachers and advisers. Diagnosis of individual difficulties and careful directing of work over long periods are to be recommended wherever possible. Classroom guidance in studying may likewise be made highly valuable. The present booklet is in no sense a substitute for these more fundamental ways of teaching students how to study. It aims to serve rather as an aid and supplement.

One word of advice is added for students who come to this booklet for help. The advice is: Use the suggestions! Merely skimming the pages which follow will do no good. Stop at every new point and inquire carefully whether the suggestion is applicable in your own studying. Figure out just how you will apply the rule; then apply it. All the rules are not equally important and all of them do not need attention from any one person. Find out which ones you need most and then hammer away persistently at those. Return to the booklet from time to time to check your methods and remind yourself of the many possibilities of improvement. Effective study methods can be made habitual only through a steady and vigorous campaign.

The student is strongly advised to go beyond the present rules and suggestions. To this end, a selected list of references for further reading is given at the end of the booklet. [Editor's note: The original bibliography has been replaced by an updated and annotated bibliography.]

A. W. K.

1

The Meaning of Study

THERE are two aims in study: one is to acquire certain bodies of knowledge; the other is to acquire certain abilities to do things. We study history to gain a knowledge of ancient Greece or of prewar Germany, whereas we study arithmetic or French to gain an ability to solve problems or read French books. Clearly, there is no sharp line between these two kinds of study. Knowledge inevitably plays some part in guiding future thought and action and is part of our ability to do. Likewise, our knowledge of how to do things and our knowledge of specific things will always affect the efficiency and ways in which we can assimilate new information.

There remains, however, a difference in emphasis between studying to acquire knowledge and studying to acquire the ability to use knowledge and to do things. With regard to studying in college, major emphasis undoubtedly belongs on the side of developing your abilities. Education should increase your powers: your abilities to work and play, vote and understand others, read and think, organize a business, plead a case, or cure a disease. This does not minimize the place of knowledge—which is in fact subordinate to the ability to use knowledge, but an indispensable subordinate. Intelligent thought and action always have sound knowledge as their basis.

One of the most valuable abilities you can develop is the *ability to study*, which is not something you do the night before an exam. Rather, you have to learn how to study so you can independently approach a novel problem and think it through to a successful solution. Mastering a method of doing something is also an accomplishment that can only be achieved through genuine study. Learning to study effectively is far more important than merely acquiring a particular body of information. In most fields, information may quickly become obsolete, whereas analyzing and approaching a problem, gathering the necessary information, and interpreting that information are skills that will not tarnish quite so quickly. Knowing how to study is tantamount to knowing how to think, observe, concentrate, organize and analyze information. It is the application of intelligence to the task of understanding and controlling the world about us. In learning to study, you are learning to think and to live. When students do not learn how to study, the biggest job of their education is left undone.

Study includes not only what you gain from books and the classroom but also what you acquire through direct observation and through actual performance. However, because it would be impossible — and too laborious — to collect stores of knowledge and points of view firsthand, studying in high school and college depends to a great extent on studying from books. Owing to this central position of books and classroom work in school study, the following pages have been limited to a discussion of these forms of learning. Nevertheless, you should continually aim to tie your book learning firmly to your everyday or firsthand experience. When you do this, the subject you are studying becomes infused with the richer meanings only your own observations and activities can bring.

In studying, as in other activities, skill is not acquired by wishing or resolving—or by reading books like this one. Rather, you must put forth a strenuous and persistent effort if results are to be achieved. Here, as elsewhere *practice* makes perfect. In other words, you must first determine where you need to improve, and then resolutely hold to the task of acquiring the methods you find outlined here. Although you may gain a certain level of comfort by reading the suggestions that follow, it is only by *using* the suggested procedures—over and over again—that you will profit from them.

2

A Fundamental Requirement
for Effective Study

THERE is one fundamental and indispensable requirement for effective study more basic than any rule or technique, and to which all specific advice concerning how to read, take notes, tackle problems, and form good study habits is secondary. This key requirement is a *driving motive*, an intense desire to learn and to achieve, an interest in things intellectual, a "will to do" in your scholastic work. If you want to learn how to study effectively, first develop a desire to master your studies and believe that you *will* master them. All else is subordinate to such spirit.

spirit
⟶

How can this spirit be acquired? First, you need to build up definite ambitions and ideals toward which your studies can lead, as well as acknowledge frankly the consequences of poor work versus the rewards of good work. Picture clearly to yourself the satisfactions of success versus the disappointments of failure. Sometimes students' attitudes are transformed from those of indifference and merely "getting by" to those of earnest and energetic effort by some emergency that causes them to think seriously about their future. Reading biographies also often helps provide the necessary spark. But the simplest and most direct stimulus to change may involve nothing more than the deliberate planning of your life. A little thought given to yourself and the things you are working for is an excellent incentive to serious study.

A second drive that makes true study possible is an interest in the subject studied. You can develop an interest in studying particular subjects if you follow these four rules:

1. **Acquire information about the subject from a variety of sources.** The more you know about a subject the easier it is to develop an interest in it. For example, it is easier to become interested in professional baseball if you learn about the players and about the fine points of the game. The same is true in every other field. Your school subjects are no exception. It is a matter of giving your interests a chance to develop by getting into the subjects.

2. **Tie the new information to your old bodies of knowledge.** Discover relations of new facts to old matters of interest. Historic events take on new interest when they are seen in relation to present issues. Physics and chemistry become more interesting to many students when they can see the application of these subjects in everyday life.

3. **Make new information personal.** Relate it to matters of real concern to you. This material on "how to study," for example, has interest for you only as you think about how it can help you.

4. **Actively use your new knowledge.** Raise questions about the points made by the book or the instructor. Anticipate what the next steps and the conclusions will be, and then check on these. Think and talk and write about the ideas; make them play a part in your actions. *Take the relevant material from one class into other classes.* Discuss difficult and questionable

points with your friends and classmates. Consider what the implications and consequences of new ideas obtained in your studies might be.

When you study with eager interest, you will discover pleasure and fascination in what you study. It is no longer work. This is the kind of studying that overcomes distractions and requires no effort or will power. It is like reading a novel or seeing a movie. The greater the proportion of your study that is of this sort the better. But the positive relationship between interest and efforts works both ways. Even when you begin studying a subject with little interest, oftentimes simply "staying with it" and trying to make it an active part of your thinking will help you develop an interest in that subject.

Although certain studies are bound to be uninteresting, especially at the beginning—and parts of these studies may continue to be uninteresting— honest efforts to master those subjects nearly always beget some level of interest. When you appreciate the necessities and rewards of effective studying, and have the will to succeed in a subject, you will rarely be disappointed. Further, several important hints can be given for gaining the decisiveness that is essential to carrying good resolutions into actual practice.

1. **Make your task definite.** Decide what is to be done and when it needs to be done. If it is discouragingly large, break the whole job up. See exactly what is involved in the first part and do that. Concentrate on a definite and manageable piece of work first, then proceed to the next.

2. **Feel intensely the urge to do the task before you.** Make clear to yourself the relation of the present task to your later studies, as well as to your larger goals and

ambitions. There are hundreds of motives for study. Bring them strongly into play.

3. **Get started at all costs.** Turn your attention away from imagined difficulties and other things that you would rather be doing. One large classification of distracting ideas consists of thoughts of other duties and of disturbing problems and queries. These can usually be shunted off by jotting them down in a notebook or on a pad of paper; most people find that writing these interfering thoughts down frees their minds from annoying tensions and real or imagined difficulties. Once freed of these interferences and irritations, you will find it easier to stay focused on the job at hand. Forget everything else. Once you get well started, you will develop interest in the subject matter itself and will no longer need to hold yourself to the work by sheer force. If you have difficulty getting down to work, a fourth rule will help.

4. **Prepare your physical world for study.** Sit down in a favorable place for studying, open your books, and take out your pencil and paper. In a word, go through the motions.

5. **Check every tendency to daydream.** Mind-wandering is a great enemy to effective study. One hour of concentrated study is worth ten with frequent lapses. Work intensely while you work. Guard vigilantly against mind-wandering, and pull yourself back sharply on every occasion. Mind-wandering is very frequently due to inadequate understanding of words or to a deficient background in the present subject. Where this is the trouble, it *always* pays to go back and provide the necessary foundation at whatever pains.

6. **Face personal problems and worries directly.** Then, either adopt the most reasonable solution you can find

or seek objective help from someone else. Worry and
personal problems are frequent causes of ineffective
study and can interfere with all sorts of other activities as well. The difficulties range from intense fears
of failure or serious misgivings about health to
troubled love affairs. Sometimes there are no completely satisfactory answers. Many young people manage either to avoid the difficulties or to meet them
without great strain. However, a certain number of
students may wish to find better ways of meeting their
personal problems. For them the following suggestions are offered:

a) *Determine as objectively and as definitely as
you can just where your problem lies.*What changes
are needed to remove the trouble, and which of the
changes *can* be made? Remember, sometimes it is
easier to alter your goals or desires than the external
conditions. In any case, the important thing is to
decide what needs to be done and also what can be
done. Even in the absence of a perfect solution,
some solutions will be better than others. Determine which is best, then plan precisely what
your course of action will involve. Then carry it
through.

b) *Find an understanding confidant who can help
you analyze and meet your difficulties.*Very often
the suggestions under (a) can best be followed by
first talking over your problems with someone in
whom you have confidence—for example, an older
friend, school adviser, psychologist, instructor, or
clergyman.

c) *Don't deceive yourself by dodging the problem
or pretending you have solved it.* For example, if social distractions prevent you from doing satisfactory

schoolwork far better to admit this fact to yourself and decide what to do about it than resort to excuses and defenses like convincing yourself that your studies "really aren't of any importance anyhow."

3

Conditions Favorable for Concentration

E FFECTIVE study demands concentration. The ability to concentrate is largely governed by your surroundings and your physical condition. Being absorbed in study is being oblivious to everything else. Learning to concentrate and study involves learning to overcome distractions. Three kinds of distractions you may face are: (1) distractions in your surroundings (noise, glare of lights, etc.), (2) distractions arising in your body (feeling of fatigue, headache, etc.), and (3) distractions in the form of irrelevant ideas. The problem of study is in no small measure the problem of dealing successfully with these distractions, which are generally best dealt with by elimination. A very few of the more important rules for eliminating these distractions are as follows:

1. **Whenever possible, study in a quiet room.** Some students find that it is necessary to eliminate visual distractions as well as noises. Others are able to tune out and thus tolerate moderate levels of distraction, whether auditory or visual, or both.

2. **See that your place of study is properly lighted, heated, and ventilated.** The light should not shine directly into your eyes or be visible out of the corner of your eye. Also, avoid a glaring reflection from the pages of your book.

3. **Arrange your chair and work to avoid strain and fatigue.** Shift your position from time to time. Be comfortable—but avoid being too comfortable. It is almost impossible to study strenuously when one is settled back in a large easychair or is reclining freely on a couch.

4. **Keep yourself in good physical condition.** Eat at regular times. Eat with your family or friends whenever you can. Make your mealtime a recreation period. Avoid heavy meals at noon and never begin study immediately after eating. Manage to get some *regular exercise and recreation.* Remember that a little regular exercise is infinitely more valuable than occasional sprees of physical activity.

5. **Get sufficient sleep so that you feel adequately rested.** Even if it means carrying fewer courses or dropping certain outside activities, it will pay in the long run to avoid cutting in on your sleep. If you have difficulty going to sleep, do something to take your mind off your work and relax before retiring. A little light reading, a warm bath, a walk, a conversation, a letter to family or friends often help. If you are bothered by sleeplessness, consult your physician.

Unfortunately, most of us do not inhabit a perfect world. Not all distractions can always be eliminated. Hence, you must learn to concentrate in spite of them. If you have developed a genuine interest in your studies, you should be able to sustain work despite minor distractions and difficulties. Nearly all of the specific suggestions throughout later chapters have a direct bearing on better concentration. Mind-wandering is after all a *symptom* of insufficient interest and poor study procedures, not the disorder itself.

4

System and Regularity in Studying

IN schoolwork, it is essential to have a plan of action. If you budget your day and then adhere to this program, you can eliminate half the effort and worry from your work. A plan that is steadily followed soon becomes the easy and natural routine of the day. Most students find it useful to have a definite *place* to study, as well as a definite time. Have a particular table and a particular chair which are always used for study and intellectual work. This place will come to *mean* study. To sit down in that particular spot and at your regular time will automatically lead you to assume a readiness for work.

The cultivation of system and regularity in work is held by many to be the secret of success. However, the details of a daily time schedule must be determined on an individual basis. Decide how many hours you will give to your studies. Avoid being too heroic in your plans. The most important first step is to make a careful estimate of your actual capacity for work. The easiest way to do this is to keep a retrospective record of your activities for a week and be sure to include information about which times are most productive.

Few students know where their time goes, so an accurate account of how your days are presently being spent is an important first step toward creating and following an effective daily schedule. At the end of the book there are convenient forms for keeping an hourly record of your week's activities. Fill in the schedule each night before retiring. You will soon gain some interesting facts about yourself and your use of time. Think over the causes of wasted time and about how you might avoid such waste in the future. You can set up a viable schedule by using the following steps:

1. **Mark off your fixed commitments on your schedule—** for example, classes, work, or clubs. How much time do you have left over? Is it enough? You can get a rough estimate of how much time you need for studying by counting the hours you used during the previous week and asking yourself whether it felt about right. Another commonly used heuristic is to multiply the number of hours you spend in class by two. Or, you might simply ask your teachers how much time they feel you should be studying for their class each week.

2. **Fill in your schedule sheet with areas designated for meals and studying.** Try to use as much time as you have available during the normal workday hours. In other words, don't plan to do all of your studying between 11 P.M. and 1 A.M.! If possible, try to select a time for intellectual work that you can use every day without interruptions. You may wish to use two or three different study periods during the day. To do so is excellent—provided you form the habit of studying regularly at these times.

3. **Make a list of all the things you will need to do within a given time period.** In general, a one-week time frame seems to work well for most college students. The rel-

evant question you might ask yourself is: What do I need to do to be able to walk into each class during the next week prepared? Don't be overly ambitious and try to plan weeks ahead just yet. Your first task is to devise a schedule that works for a week.

4. **Break down each task on your list into smaller tasks.** The amount of time to be given to each subject must also be settled, as must the order in which you tackle your studies. You cannot, of course, determine in advance exactly how long each assignment will require or at what time precisely you can take up the next. But it is best to plan the approximate time for your assignments and the order in which you will do them. You can, in this way, entirely avoid the serious difficulties of "not knowing what to do first" and of worrying about the other things you "ought to be doing."

5. **Distribute your tasks among the empty spaces on your schedule.** Keep some time unscheduled so that you can deal with the unexpected. What you will have then is a preliminary blueprint for the week to come, which should be flexible enough to allow you to rearrange some units when necessary. Remember, you will be more likely to lose control of your new schedule if it is packed too tightly. Your schedule should also allow you to take time off from your studies. In fact, you can use the promise of planned recreational activities as a reward to help motivate your adherence to a schedule. Try to work hard when you work and play hard when you play!

6. **Keep a record of what you actually do.** Use the knowledge you gain in so doing to create your schedule for the next week. Always give yourself credit for gradual

movement toward your goals. Be realistic! For example, if you find that you never work produc-
tively at a particular hour, try reorganizing your
expectations so as to take that idiosyncrasy into
account.

5

Reading Effectively

F OR many high-school and college students, reading still means beginning with the first word of a text and reading word by word until its end, which is not always the most productive way to read. Rather, an assignment is usually easier to master when you combine a preliminary rapid survey with a more careful and thoughtful second reading of the text. Some students find it helpful to think in terms of reading in layers—first for the gist and overall structure, only later filling in the details in one or more subsequent readings. Contrary to expectations, when a detailed understanding of the text is needed, multiple readings generally take less time than does a single word-by-word reading of the material.

Reading for the Big Picture

Reading for the big picture is an important part of reading effectively. Some general rules for how to get the big picture in what you read are as follows.

1. **Think about the topic of study before beginning to read.** How does this reading fit into the work of the course? How is it related to preceding topics? What problem is it trying to answer? How much do you already know about this subject? Try to recall informa-

tion from your previous readings, study, and experiences that bears upon the reading at hand.

2. **Formulate questions that can guide your reading.** Writing these questions down is an efficient way of keeping them in mind as you read. Think about how *you* would develop the subject.

3. **Obtain a preliminary rapid impression of a book.** Note the title, the author, the author's position and titles of other writings, the year the book was written, the preface, the table of contents, and the manner of presentation. Form an idea of the value of the book or article. Decide what you expect it to give you. Note the author's plan and keep this in mind as you read. Try to form an idea of the author's main argument.

4. **Read rapidly through the whole assignment.** Neglect for now the more minor details. Rather, notice the places where major new topics are introduced and where especially important thoughts are summarized. Get the "lay of the land" and the natural division of the territory covered. With a little practice you can learn to read very quickly through even long assignments and grasp the main ideas. In many books you will find a number of examples given to illustrate each principle. Once you are certain you understand the principle, the examples need not detain you.

5. **Go beyond the book.** Forge new links and create new examples. Treat the author critically. Try challenging the main ideas being presented and then imagine how the author(s) might meet such challenges. Tie the present discussion to your previous thinking in the subject. Make it part of *your* thinking. *Use* the material in your conversations and discussions. (The next section

in this chapter deals in greater detail with methods to be used in thorough reading.)

6. **Make note of the important points as you read.** Mark your book or take notes. You can use these notes later when you review the material. When you come to an important point, you should mark it or jot it down in your notebook. At the end of each paragraph or set of paragraphs, stop and think over what you have read, then summarize the essential point(s) in a brief note. Note taking is valuable both at the time you think through and record the points and at later times when you wish to review or refer to the topic.

7. **Review your notes before proceeding to read your new assignment each day.** This requires only a few minutes and is extraordinarily valuable. If your notes are not perfectly clear, return to the original reading and re-fresh your memory. When you use your notes in this way, you will be more likely to build each lesson on a sound foundation.

8. **Be self-critical about your acquisitions of knowledge.** Many students are too easily satisfied with them-selves. While you cannot hope to learn a great deal about any subject in a short time, see that the little you do learn is clear and definite. Above everything else, do not blithely accept vague and muddy ideas. The habit of getting "smatterings" of subjects spells intellectual ruin. It is generally far better to get a *few fundamental ideas* from a course or a book—and understand them clearly—than to get scores of "half-baked" notions.

Once you have completed these steps, you will find that the details are far more meaningful and more readily grasped. As you move on to the next stage of reading for details, keep the main idea in mind and try to relate all the subordinate points to this central thought. Parts of a reading which by themselves may seem obscure and difficult become clear when they are related to the underlying idea. Knowing what comes later can save you many minutes of perplexity and mind-wandering.

Reading for Details

It is almost always desirable to skim through a book or assignment hurriedly before tackling it in a thoroughgoing fashion. If the book is not of much value, the preliminary reading suffices. If it is worth a more careful reading, the rapid survey will be most helpful in giving the essential ideas and point of view into which the detailed subject matter can be fitted.

It is assumed, moreover, that even before you skim a book or article you will perform the indispensable preparations. That is, you should: (1) *think* about the topic and formulate questions and problems which the reading is to solve; (2) glance over your notes from previous reading and class discussion that bear upon, or lead up to, this subject; (3) become familiar with the book or article by finding out something of the author and the nature of this piece of writing.

After all these preparations are completed, you are ready to read the matter thoroughly, which can be accomplished using the following steps.

1. **Keep the purpose of the reading in mind as you read.**
   See how the points fit in with the main purpose and support it. When you find your mind wandering, stop and recall your problem, relating it to the passage you are reading.

2. **Be sure you have the main thought of each paragraph.**
   Stop at the end of each paragraph or division and recall
   in your own words the central thought of that section.
   Ask yourself questions about it. What relation does it
   bear to the main problem and to the points that pre-
   cede it? If the paragraph is not clear, go back and read
   each sentence alone. If a sentence is not clear, take
   each phrase and word. Be sure you know the meanings
   of the words you encounter, extend your vocabulary at
   every opportunity. If you are certain you understand
   the main thought of the paragraph, however, do not
   waste your time on single phrases and sentences save
   to note technical terms which will be needed later.

   Stopping to recall what you have just read is the
   best way to be sure that you are getting the thought.
   Although stopping to recall information as you read
   may appear to waste time, it actually has been demon-
   strated to add greatly to efficiency in study. Even when
   you are pressed for time, stop frequently in your
   studying to think over and check yourself on what you
   have read.

3. **Vary the rate of your reading.** Read the important and
   difficult points slowly, making sure you understand
   them. Read the familiar points more rapidly. Skip over
   the points that have no significance for your present
   purpose. The secret of study is to seize upon the important and the difficult parts and concentrate upon
   them.

4. **Think critically as you read.** Draw your own conclusions. Go beyond the book. Spend time thinking over
   the material you read rather than merely memorizing
   the points. Too many students accept blindly as truth
   whatever they see on a printed page. A safer attitude is
   one that carefully weighs and considers the facts,

opinions, and theories that are read. Nothing is true simply because it is in a book. Nor is it either true or false merely because it fits in—or fails to fit in—with your previous notions. Above everything else, cultivate an open-minded attitude toward the subject you are reading. Be ready to believe, but not too ready. Examine the evidence and the reasoning behind an author's conclusions. When you are not convinced, be willing to suspend judgment.

In thinking over what you are reading, ask yourself such questions as: Is the writer citing facts accurately? Does he or she distinguish between facts and opinions? Do the conclusions follow necessarily from the evidence? Do these conclusions agree with your own independent views? By considering these questions you will come to conclusions of your own, whether they happen to agree with the author's or not. Be sure, however, to view your own conclusions as tentative and subject to change.

As you read and think, you must do more than arrive at critical conclusions. Find illustrations and applications of the points being made. Consider what further conclusions might follow. What are the implications of the author's view? What light does this reading throw on other problems you have been struggling with? In short, let your new reading continually stimulate thought on a host of related topics.

5. **Record the main thought of each division of your reading.** Mark the important points in the reading as you come to them (only when it is your own book, of course). The simplest way of marking the passages is to draw a line beside them. If the passage is especially important, draw a double line beside it. Use an interrogation mark beside points which you are not sure

about, or where you wish to make further inquiries. Other special marks may be adopted at will, but it is important to have a uniform system in all your reading. If you do not own the book, record your notes in a loose-leaf notebook or use Post-Its, which are removable, to flag important sections.

At the end of each paragraph or section, when you stop to think over what you have read, summarize the central idea by means of a brief marginal note or by marking the author's own summary statement. Also, record questions that occur to you and points where you take issue with the writer. When you take critical notes and mark passages, you are forced to think and to pick out the essential points.

6. **Make a mental (or written) outline of the material as you read; then review the entire reading with this outline in mind.** The thoughts of the different sections must be interrelated. Organize the material into main points and subordinate points. Obtain a clear picture of the *entire* topic. Try to connect the details to the big picture you formed earlier. A jumble of disconnected facts and opinions is useless. Group the details under the important thoughts. Think over the reading point by point with your outline as a guide. Change the outline if necessary. In the end, be sure that you see the subject as an organized whole.

7. **Organize your notes under major questions, and do your reviewing by repeatedly testing yourself on these questions.** This method of "self-recitation," properly used, can contribute immensely to the efficiency of your study periods. Formulate one or two questions on each section of your reading—questions which go to the heart of the subject being discussed. Write these questions in your notebook, and under each one, then,

list briefly the essential points that will answer the
question. When you review the material—both immediately after reading and later—ask yourself each
question. Keep the answers covered as you review. See
how well you can recall the essential points bearing
on that question. Then check your answer against
your notes. Wherever necessary, go back to the book to
refresh and enrich your thinking on the specific points.

In addition to the foregoing, also test yourself to
see if you can recall all the *questions* that relate to
the major topic under consideration. Keep reviewing
the questions and retesting yourself until you have a
completely organized picture in mind. In this self-
recitation process you should also go beyond the
book by asking yourself what *other questions* are relevant and what *other evidence* should be considered
on each question. Insert these supplementary and
critical thoughts into your notes in parentheses, or
with your initials, to distinguish them from the author's ideas.

Speed Reading

When students express concerns about their
reading—especially when those concerns first
emerge in college—what they often really want to
know is: How can I read faster? This question most
commonly arises when students realize that they
must read tremendous amounts of material in a
short period of time. The most obvious solution they
think would be to read more rapidly, which they
often assume has something to do with changing the
pattern of their eye movements during reading. In
truth, much of what these students really hope to accomplish has less to do with what they do with their

eyes than with what they do with their minds. Ironically, a crucial factor in how quickly and efficiently they can read is the extent to which and how they prepare their minds for reading. The essence of what they need to accomplish was discussed earlier in the section about "Reading for the Big Picture" and merits repeating and embellishment here.

A good reader is one who knows how and when to vary their approach to reading. Learn to skip wisely. "Hit the high spots." Do not be afraid to skip phrases, sentences, and even whole paragraphs, provided you have caught the drift of the author's thought. (Remember that you are going to reread the matter if it is something to be mastered.) Give special attention to the beginning and end of each sentence and each paragraph. Often you need only the first and last sentence of a paragraph to get the whole thought. Authors have different habits in this matter, and you will do well to discover in each assignment whether summary sentences are used and whether they ordinarily occur at the beginning or the end of paragraphs. When a book has printed marginal notes or paragraph headings or a detailed table of contents, you can use these to great advantage in skimming the book.

The important thing to strive for is to read initially as quickly as you can in order to get an overview of the material. This overview will provide you with the kinds of structure that make it easier to master the details quickly and efficiently. Put simply, if you know where you are going as you begin a thorough reading of the material, you will read more efficiently.

6

Listening and Note Taking

THE classroom is a place to learn, not a place to demonstrate what you have already learned. Aside from your reading, the most important part of your studying is in the classroom. You need to form good classroom habits as well as good reading habits. When you are planning your strategies for classroom participation and note taking, it is crucial that you first *ascertain the teaching method in each of your classes and then guide your activities accordingly.* Different classes are conducted in different ways, and you will need to adopt methods appropriate to each of your classes. The contrast is especially striking between the lecture method and the discussion method. But beyond this broad division there are many other variations— including differences in the kinds of lectures and discussions, and differences in the personalities and the requirements of the instructors. Lectures may be presentations of material that is not in your books; they may supplement your texts; or they may merely repeat, in different form, what you have read. Again, they may aim primarily to present problems, applications, and criticisms of your reading; or they may be principally inspirational and stimulating. Obviously your method of listening and note taking will differ in each case.

Similar variety exits in classes not given over to lectures. Some instructors may quiz you or expect you to contribute to the discussion without being questioned. Some will only discuss points on which you have already prepared, while others will discuss matters that are not in your regular assignments. In order to profit fully from your classroom work, you must be aware of all these possibilities and adapt yourself to the methods being used.

Despite this diversity of classroom work, some rules can be laid down that are of general applicability and are similar to the rules for effective reading.

1. **Before class, think about the subject matter.** Prepare your mind. Recall the main points of your reading. Review your notes from the day before. Think of the questions and problems that arose during your preparation of the assigned material. The minutes preceding the class hour can be used to excellent advantage for thinking over the topic as a whole and for formulating the difficulties and the issues of the subject.

2. **During class, think all around the points raised in the lecture or discussion.** Go beyond that which is presented. Keep recalling related points from your reading and experience. Tie together ideas that have been drifting about. Think critically of the conclusions and views that are expressed. Ask questions. Make each idea prove its soundness.

   Above everything, be *active* in your listening. Passive absorption is impossible. The capable listener thinks far ahead of the speaker. Train yourself to anticipate what is coming. Debate mentally with the speaker. Try to find the weak point in each argument. Pick out the essential ideas and link them to your previous thinking in the subject. If the discussion is dull and uninteresting, occupy your thinking with a deeper and broader inquiry into the topic. Good students do some of their most penetrating and creative thinking during the "dry" parts of their classes.

3. **Concentrate on the topic of discussion.** Check every tendency toward mind-wandering. Pull yourself back sharply when your mind rambles off to irrelevant matters. The best way to avoid daydreaming and wandering attention is to follow the advice of rule 2. Keep your mind active with thoughts about the subject being presented. Note taking will also aid in combating tendencies toward mind-wandering. But the greatest thing is your earnest effort.

4. **Take notes on the important points.** The kind of notes you take will be determined in large measure by the nature of your classroom work. Along these lines, a few hints that may be helpful are as follows.

    a) *When the class period is devoted to questions and discussions, take relatively few notes and fit these into your reading notes.* Usually you will need to jot down only the conclusions of a discussion or a few words to indicate the answer to a problem that has bothered you. These notes can often be placed to best advantage directly in your book, beside the question or a paragraph to which they refer. If the instructor ordinarily summarizes long discussions or adds new material to that of the book, you may find it valuable to take notes on cards or in a notebook. Avoid long notes. Keep your attention free for thought on the subjects discussed. Thinking through a problem yourself is infinitely better than getting someone else's answer neatly written in your notes.

b) *Where the lecture method is used, you will need to take more notes than in the case of class discussions.* How detailed your notes need to be will depend upon the kind of lecture and upon your own best method of study. In general, make your notes as brief as is practicable. Keep your mind free to think over the points of the lecture. Understanding the lecture clearly is your primary aim; notes are secondary.

If a lecture is clearly organized, cast your notes directly into the form of the lecture. Some instructors may give you an outline of their points, or present the subject in such clear-cut divisions that you can easily form an outline. Your notes should be a skeleton of the lecture. Arrange main heads and subheads in accordance with some definite plan and system of symbols. If the lectures follow a syllabus fairly closely, it is a good plan to write the notes directly in the syllabus. It is wise to go over your notes soon after they are taken. Think about the points and how they interrelate, then make the necessary revisions. Remember, even if the lecture is clear at the time, it will be forgotten very quickly unless you have notes which you can review later.

Many lectures do not fall into a clear outline form. Often the best you can do is to jot down important or striking points in the order in which they are mentioned, even though they do not fit into a general scheme. With notes of this sort you will find it especially important to rewrite and to organize the material very soon after the lecture. While the points are still fresh in your thinking, the notes will have meaning and can be written up in full; a day or two later they will be of little use.

5. **Each day after class, read over your notes and think about the points that were made.** Pay particular attention to the points where your class notes agree and disagree with the reading and your previous impressions. Follow up each point that is not entirely clear, through further reading, thinking, discussion, and consultation with the instructor. Remember, your notes are useful only to the extent that you can put meaning into them. The way to make notes meaningful is to work over them carefully and thoroughly while the material is still fresh and easily recalled.

7

Aids in Memorizing

MEMORIZING a lesson is often contrasted with mastering it. Thinking and memory are frequently viewed as alternatives, which can be misleading. Understanding a point always involves remembering related ideas and facts. In order to think, you must have some materials of thought—materials furnished by memory. Remembering the significant points of a lesson is a necessary part of mastering it.

The common feeling against mere memory in study arises because memory is thought of as mechanical and related to rote learning, or learning by heart. But this is only part—and the less important part—of what is involved in memory. Memory of connected and meaningful ideas, of material that has been understood and thought about, is clearly a most important part of all effective study. A lesson is never mastered without a great deal of remembering—logical remembering.

Thinking is given first place in discussions of how to study and memory is little mentioned simply because remembering takes care of itself. Memory, in short, is a by-product of thoughtful study. *The rules that previous chapters have given for improving methods of reading and learning are at the same time rules for improving your memory.* The only way that improvements can be made in memory, as a matter of fact, is through the use of better methods of learning.

Here are some brief rules for improving your ability to remember:

1. **Get the meaning of the idea to be remembered.** Make sure that you clearly understand the material. Think about it and tie it to as many other ideas as you can. Form a variety of associations among the ideas. Look at the new material from all sides. Think of illustrations and applications of the facts and principles; inquire into causes and effects. See if there are exceptions or difficulties. The richer the associations, the better the memory.

2. **Go over the material to be remembered again and again.** Repetition of ideas strengthens the associations among them. The stronger the associations, the better the memory.

3. **Avoid mechanical repetition.** Think about the material you are trying to learn each time you go over it. Take notes and talk to yourself or to a fellow student about it. Merely going over the words will not help you remember. Bring yourself back sharply when you begin drifting in this passive fashion.

4. **Learn with the intention of recalling.** You can remember better if you study with a definite expectation of recalling or using what you are studying. Study with the intention to remember for permanent use, not simply for recitation the next day.

5. **Stop frequently during your studying and recall the things you are learning.** A large part of your study time should be spent in recalling the ideas you have read. When you cannot recall, turn back and refresh your memory. Then, practice recalling the whole topic

again. Repeat this process until you have really mastered the material.

6. **Have confidence in your ability to remember.** Forgetting is often due to a lack of confidence. After you have once mastered a topic, trust yourself to remember it. The confidence itself will help.

7. **If necessary, form arbitrary associations to help you remember information with no logical connection.** The need for this is rare. Most facts worth remembering can be organized into some logical and sensible form. These meaningful or logical associations are critical for effective recall. In remembering names and numbers, however, logical connections are often absent. Many memory aids and devices have been proposed for such matters (jingles for the number of days in the months, and for names of the presidents, etc.). But advertised "memory training systems" typically have elaborate codes which are usually far more trouble than they are worth. Your own self-made associations are more economical.

8

Cramming and Examinations

CRAMMING is good or bad depending on what is meant by it. If it refers to feverish last-minute efforts to memorize masses of material which should have been learned during the course, it is decidedly harmful and serves only to give you some confused smatterings of the subject. The fragments of knowledge that are acquired in this eleventh-hour dash will be quickly forgotten and are of little lasting use. Cramming is no substitute for faithful daily work during the course.

If cramming is interpreted as meaning a strenuous review at the close of a course, it has much to recommend it. You can do a great deal to refresh your memory and to note the interrelations of topics by running over the main ideas that have been dealt with. If you have notes from your books and class discussions, use these in review. If your notes are not adequate, skim through your textbook to get a bird's-eye view of the course. Then think over each main topic, try to recall as much as you can, and turn to the book for further light when necessary. Two now familiar rules are especially important:

1. **Review the main points, get a skeleton view of the subject, and avoid memorizing scattered details.** Get the main ideas and think about these long enough to see how the details are to be organized under them.

The specific examples and facts will be readily recalled if you are clear about the way they fit into general conclusions and points of view.

2. **Give yourself plenty of time to review.** Avoid high-pressure reviewing at the last minute. Do your reviewing early. Begin reviewing the whole course at least a week or two before examinations. Leave only a few finishing touches for the day before the examinations.

When preparing for and taking examinations, it may also be useful to keep the following advice in mind:

1. **Try to determine the nature of the examination and the ground it will cover.** Often instructors will provide this information ahead of time, perhaps when they announce the date of an exam. If not, you might, for example, talk with students who have taken the course in previous years.

2. **Think about the kinds of questions that might be asked.** Plan how you would answer them. What has the instructor stressed during the course and in previous examinations? What questions would you ask if you were giving the examination? What questions do your fellow students expect?

3. **When you go to take the exam, be well rested, and remain as calm and self-confident as possible.** If you have reviewed carefully and have a general understanding of the course, you should be reassured that you will do well.

4. **During the exam, read over the whole set of examination questions and think about each one long enough to understand it.** The questions often have some relation to one another and your ideas on one question may help with another question. Also be sure you observe general directions pertaining to the examination as a whole.

5. **Read each question very carefully before beginning to answer it.** Make certain that you understand the real point of the question. Think around it for a time before deciding finally how to approach it.

6. **Make written outlines of your answers.** Outlining will help you immensely in getting a complete and rounded answer to each question. A well-organized answer also does wonders in convincing the instructor that you have mastered the topic.

7. **Reserve time to go over your answers and make necessary changes.** When rereading your examination, you will be able to catch places during the exam where you did not make your meaning clear, as well as places where you can add to the thought or modify it to your advantage.

9

Putting One's Knowledge
to Use

ONLY one general rule is set forth in this chapter, but it is the most important of all rules for effective study. Briefly, it is this:

Study actively. Learn by doing. Use your knowledge by thinking, talking, and writing about the things you are learning.

If you are asked why you study, your obvious answer is that your studies will be useful because you will profit by the knowledge and the work habits that you acquire. You will apply the things you learn, not merely in making a success of your vocation, but also in all your thinking, talking, and writing, and in conduct of the most varied sorts. When you think through new problems or draw new conclusions, you are using your knowledge. Similarly, when you give advice or information to or discuss issues with your friends and when you write, plan, or take action in social and political affairs—in everything you do— you are using your knowledge. The one great aim of all your study is increased efficiency of thought and action through putting your knowledge and skill to use.

Using knowledge is not only the aim of your studying; it is *the very essence of the study process.*

Knowledge is not something that you can absorb and hold for later use. Knowledge is acquired only through thinking and doing. The material in books becomes part of your mental equipment only when you succeed in tying it to the rest of your knowledge and *use* your ideas in relation to one another.

The common saying "We learn through doing" says it all. Learning is an *active* process. In order to acquire new ideas, you must react to them, put them to use, talk and write about them, and act upon them.

A few specific bits of advice that will help you follow the general rule of learning by doing:

1. **Think of illustrations and concrete examples to which your new knowledge applies.** Ideas that you read or hear will remain empty words unless you connect them with familiar concrete contents. In studying continually force yourself to find specific illustrations and applications.

2. **Compare new ideas with the knowledge you already have.** Criticize and evaluate opposed views. Use the new material in reexamining your earlier conclusions. You can make ideas part of your own thinking by using them to mold and polish other ideas. Your knowledge in this way becomes tested and sound.

3. **Use your knowledge to explain facts and to foresee consequences.** Consider how other facts are causally related to the present one. Interrelate and organize your knowledge. Think of the causes and probable consequences of the facts you are studying. The habit of using new ideas to look ahead and to help you think through the logical implications of facts is a most important way of putting your knowledge to use.

4. **Put your ideas on paper.** Make outlines. Write essays. Draw diagrams. *Writing is one important aid in studying.* It also affords a valuable way to use your ideas. Many people do their best thinking in the process of putting their thoughts on paper.

5. **Talk over the things you are learning with others—in class discussions, with your classmates and instructors, or even with family and friends.** Talking often helps remarkably in clarifying ideas. Find someone with whom you can talk over the main points of your study. Teaching a subject is said to be the best way of learning it. Find someone to whom you can explain the matters you are learning.

6. **Apply your knowledge.** Put the principles you learn into practice. An excellent example is the material contained in this booklet. Knowledge of how to study is worthless unless you *use* the ideas to improve your actual study methods. In all your studying, adopt the policy of applying your knowledge as much as possible—and as soon as possible.

10

Summary of Rules for Effective Study

THE more important rules and suggestions contained in the preceding chapters are briefly restated here. Stop and think carefully of each point. Ask yourself: Do I follow this suggestion in my studying? When you come to a rule that you have not been applying, take special note of it and refer to the chapter where it was discussed. It takes time to form good habits of study; you must hammer away steadily to produce results.

It will happen, however, if you persistently apply the following rules:

1. Feel intensely the desire to master your studies and resolve that you *will* master them. Build up definite ambitions; appreciate your duties and responsibilities; recognize the consequences of poor work and the rewards of good work.
2. Carry your resolutions into practice. The following methods will help:

    a) Think frankly of the larger consequences of success or failure in the task before you.

    b) Make your task definite and keep this one job clearly in the center of your attention.

    c) Get set for study. Begin work! Go through the motions.

    d) Concentrate on the subject. Check every tendency to daydream. Guard against mind-wandering and pull yourself back sharply on every occasion.

e) *Face* your personal problems that interfere with studying. Meet them intelligently instead of continuing to fret and worry over them. Seek wise counsel from trusted friends or advisers. Guard against deceiving yourself with make-believe solutions and self-defensive explanations.

3. Develop interest in your subjects of study. To do this:
   a) Acquire information about the subject.
   b) Tie the new information to old matters of interest.
   c) Make the new material *personal*. Relate it to matters of concern to *you*.
   d) Take an *active* attitude toward the subject and *use* the new knowledge.
4. Avoid all distractions that interfere with your studying—noise, glare of lights, uncomfortable feelings, strains, too great relaxation, and so on.
5. Arrange a fixed daily program of study. Plan your work. Cultivate systematic habits as regards the time and the place for your studies.
6. Develop effective methods of reading.
   a) Think about the topic of study before beginning to read. Prepare your mind. Review your notes from the day before.
   b) Obtain a preliminary impression of a book or other reading by referring to the preface, table of contents, etc.
   c) Read rapidly through your assignment first, to get a bird's-eye view of the whole by:
   (1) Reading phrases and sentences, not words.
   (2) Skipping wisely; reading only parts of sentences and paragraphs.
   d) Read your assignment a second time, more slowly, thoroughly, and thoughtfully. Some specific rules are:

(1) Keep the purpose and plan of the reading in mind as you read.

(2) Stop at the end of each paragraph and *think* about the point. Look at the ideas from all sides. Be sure you have a clear understanding of the thought. Learn the meanings of new or unfamiliar words.

(3) Read important and difficult points slowly. Read the familiar and unimportant points rapidly.

(4) Think critically while you read. Draw your own conclusions. Go beyond the book.

e) Make note of important points in your reading. Mark your book or take notes. Summarize the principal thoughts and jot them down. Use your notes in reviewing each day.

f) Make a mental or written outline of the whole reading. Think over this organized outline of the topic before leaving the book or reading. For thorough mastery, organize your notes under major *questions.* Then review the reading by testing yourself on these questions until your "self-recitation" is satisfactory.

g) Be certain your knowledge is clear and well thought through. Avoid vague and muddy thinking. Get a few fundamental ideas *clearly.*

7. Develop effective methods of classroom work.

a) Ascertain the teaching method in each of your classes and guide your classroom activities accordingly.

b) Think about the subject matter for the day, before class. Prepare your mind. Review the work of the preceding day.

c) During the class period consider all aspects of the points raised in the lecture or discussion. Go beyond the ideas presented.

d) Concentrate on the general topic of discussion. Check every tendency toward mind-wandering or daydreaming.

e) Take notes on the important points. But remember that the first thing is to *understand* the ideas; getting them down on paper is secondary.

(1) During discussions, take relatively few notes and fit these into your reading notes.

(2) During lectures, get a skeleton outline of the lecture or a set of notes covering the main points. Revise your notes while the subject matter is still fresh in your thinking.

f) Use your notes after class each day. Think over points which are not clear and seek further light from books and from your instructor.

8. Improve your ability to remember by adopting better methods of learning. Specifically—

a) Get the *meaning* of the idea to be remembered.

b) Go over the material to be remembered again and again.

c) Keep actively attentive; avoid mechanical repetitions.

d) Learn with the intention of recalling.

e) Stop frequently during your studying and make yourself recall the things you are learning.

f) Have confidence in your ability to remember.

g) When facts have no logical connection, form some arbitrary associations to help remember them.

9. In preparing for examinations—

a) Review the main points; get a skeleton view of the subject. Avoid memorizing scattered details.

b) Do your reviewing early. Avoid high-pressure cramming at the last minute.

    c) Find out from the instructor what kind of examination will be given and the ground it will cover. Anticipate as well as you can the kinds of questions which will be asked.

10. In taking examinations—

    a) Be well rested. Remain as calm and self-confident as possible. Trust your memory.

    b) Read over the whole set of examination questions and think about each one long enough to understand it.

    c) Read each question very carefully before beginning to answer it.

    d) Make mental or written outlines of your answers.

    e) Go over your answers if you have time and make necessary changes.

11. Study actively. *Use* your knowledge by thinking, talking, and writing about the things you are learning. *Apply your knowledge as much as possible and as soon as possible.*

Bibliography

Adler, Mortimer J. *How to Speak How to Listen*. N.Y.: Macmillan, 1985.

    Meant to be a companion to *How to Read a Book*. It is a thorough and provocative discussion of the underlying factors that can and do make communication successful. I never used it with students, but expect that it would be highly interesting to those with a special interest in effective communication.

Adler, Mortimer J. and Van Doren, Charles. *How to Read a Book*. N.Y.: Simon and Schuster, 1972.

    A true classic, first published in 1940, this is the most interesting and comprehensive book about serious reading and how to do it well that I have found. For several years, I sent students off to Harper Library to borrow a well-worn copy of an earlier edition. Then, I discovered this revised edition. Not an especially short book, but one well worth serious browsing. Includes some interesting and useful advice about speed reading.

Bransford, John D. and Stein, Barry S. *The Ideal Problem Solver: A Guide for Improving Thinking, Learning, and Creativity*. N.Y.: W. H. Freeman, 1984.

    An interesting, easy to read approach for dealing with problems of every sort creatively and productively.

Burka, Jane B. and Yuen, Lenora M. *Procrastination: Why You Do It, What to Do about It*. Reading, Mass.: Addison-Wesley, 1983.

    This could be a taxing book to read, but it's not! Whether you are trying to understand or overcome procrastination, you will more than likely find it useful and even amusing. Sound, practical advice that really works, if you get around to using it. Even if you don't, it is an enjoyable read. This book was always out on loan.

Kelsch, Mary Lynn and Kelsch, Thomas. *Writing Effectively: A Practical Guide.* Englewood Cliffs, N.J.: Prentice-Hall, 1981.

A great book for getting started when the words just won't flow. A simple, straightforward treatment that seems to work effectively with young as well as more mature writers. Many students find the sections dealing with identifying and developing controlling ideas especially valuable.

Pauk, Walter. *How to Study in College* (4th ed.). Boston, Mass.: Houghton Mifflin, 1989.

This book offers a comprehensive and detailed discussion of a range of study skills, many of which are not treated here. The section on speed reading is quite good. Although the advice Pauk offers is not radically different from that which Kornhauser offers, he expands nicely on these fundamental points, gives exercises to follow, and explains why the different strategies work.

Strunk, William and White, E. B. *Elements of Style* (3d ed.). N.Y.: Macmillan, 1979.

This persistent little classic deserves to be on every student's bookshelf. With unparalleled economy it covers the basics of writing clearly. Its straightforward and easy to use style appeals to students in all disciplines. Students in the physical sciences seem especially delighted by its simplicity and brevity.

Williams, Joseph M. *Style: Toward Clarity and Grace.* Chicago: University of Chicago Press, 1990.

This book provides an excellent approach for thinking about and revising prose. The real power—and beauty—of this book is that it provides not only a system for revising but also a basis for understanding why and how a particular text does, or does not, work. In a sense then, this is really a toolkit for mending prose. Students and professionals with a fair amount of experience writing but who wish to gain greater control of their prose style find it especially useful.

[Editor's note: This list does not represent a systematic search of the how-to-study literature. It is, for the most part, simply a selection of those books I found to be most practical and helpful in working with students in the College. The inclusion of a book means that in my experience students have consistently found it useful.]

What I Plan to Do: The Blueprint

	MON	TUES	WED	THUR	FRI	SAT	SUN
7 A.M.							
8 A.M.							
9 A.M.							
10 A.M.							
11 A.M.							
12 noon							
1 P.M.							
2 P.M.							
3 P.M.							
4 P.M.							
5 P.M.							
6 P.M.							
7 P.M.							
8 P.M.							
9 P.M.							
10 P.M.							
11 P.M.							
12 P.M.							

What I Did Do: Retrospective Record

	MON	TUES	WED	THUR	FRI	SAT	SUN
7 A.M.							
8 A.M.							
9 A.M.							
10 A.M.							
11 A.M.							
12 noon							
1 P.M.							
2 P.M.							
3 P.M.							
4 P.M.							
5 P.M.							
6 P.M.							
7 P.M.							
8 P.M.							
9 P.M.							
10 P.M.							
11 P.M.							
12 P.M.							